LOVES MELTING POT

Inspirational Romance Compilation

By: Lawander D. Harris

COPYRIGHT PAGE

Title

LOVES MELTING POT
Inspirational Romance Compilation

By Lawander D. Harris

ISBN: 978-1-105-74455-6

Printed by: Lulu Book Publishing,

– In the United States of America –

CONTENTS PAGE

STORY ONE

LOVES PROMISE

"WHO COULD HAVE GUESSED THAT THE ROAD FULL OF SADNESS AND PROMISES WOULD LEAD MIA TO LOVE?"

It had only been six months since young Mia's father had passed away. Her mother had used all the insurance money on medical procedures. She'd hoped to buy more time with Booker Truth, her loving husband of thirty-five wonderful years. But now they were just about flat broke. With under a thousand dollars in the bank, Bethany sat in the chair in her quiet room that afternoon and prayed. She asked God to send help for her and Mia; specifically, someone to take care of her teenager, after she was no longer able and when she was gone. Feeling assured of her prayer, Bethany left it in the care of the one who watches. She then left that room and headed to the kitchen to finish evening dinner. "Mom, I'm home," Mia yelled into the kitchen. "Yes honey, I know." "How was your day?" "Groovy!" "That's wonderful dear. Did anything new or different happen to you today?" "No mom, just the same old routine ...you

know." Mia was very close to her mom. And they often had these pulsating conversations. "Now wash up and set the table please." That evening while at dinner, Bethany wondered if it was the right time to share the unpleasant news with her daughter of her new diagnosis.

With her father Booker gone and now looking at losing a mother within less than a year, seemed too much a burden for a seventeen year old. Bethany had come to the decision to move back to her home town, where at least she could be around long unheard from relatives, if something happened to her sooner than predicted. Within three months the team of two had settled down in the little town of Gilford, New Hampshire and life moved forward. One day Mia had gone to the pharmacy to pick-up her mom's medicine. "Thank you Sally," Mia said, leaving the customer-service window. "Wow... who was that?" Young twenty-four year old, Zeth Kilroy's ear, had caught Mia's charming voice. Leaning her head towards his, cupping her hands to her mouth... "Her name's Mia Jayree Truth," Sally whispered. "She's new in town, but her mother grew up here." "I'm in love," Zeth teased. Sally chuckled. Every week thereafter, Mia arrived like clock-work to pick up her ill mothers prescription. And Zeth just took note of her every time, admiring her pleasant way and soothing voice. He never once said anything, nor did he approach her, but just adored her. Each night he arrived home and sat alone in the big mansion he'd inherited from his great-great grandfather. Zeth was the fifth generation of pharmaceutical billionaires. But you'd not have known it by his modest behaviors and generous spirit. In Fact, young 25 year old Zeth set on a board of directors who helped manage Pam's Pharmacy. His store, named after his mom. The same store, Mia came to everyday to pick up medical products.

A six month period had gone by and Bethany grew worse. But Mia made her mom a promise to stay committed to finishing high school and letting the distant spirited relatives help her. Especially, since she'd be eighteen next year. She figured after that, she could get out of this small town that showed no promise. Curious to know more, Zeth secretly inquire further into Mia's situation. When he found out about her ill mother, he made arrangements to help in every way he could, favoring Mia and her mom with extra medical supplies and some free medicine. Equally, offering to deliver these items himself. To Mia's surprise, the knock that came at the door that evening would be the one divine appointment that would change her circumstances forever. "Hello," she said, opening the front screen door. "Greetings to you lovely lady, I'm Zeth, the delivery guy from the Pharmacy." He responded. "These are for your

Mother." Mia didn't' know what to think or say. Standing there ...mouth open, mesmerized by his modest gentle gesture. Once she unlocked her eyes from his, she thanked the kind handsome man, said good night, and went back to caring for her mom. It had now been a year since Mia's mom, Bethany had deceased. And Mia was just fine in the absence of both her parents. It appears all promises of commitment had been kept. Mia kept her word of promise to her mom and did graduate. Bethany got her prayer promise from God that he wouldn't leave young Mia alone. Plus the providential meeting of Zeth, Pharmaceutical king of Gilford, would be keeping his promise of commitment to marry Mia, in two short years when she was twenty. Who could have guessed that the road full of sadness and promises would lead Mia to love?

Inspirational Romance

STORY TWO

THE FIXER UPPER

"I'D GOTTEN LOST SOMEWHERE BETWEEN HER HELLO AND THE HAZEL HUES IN HER EYES."

It was just the other day Joseph was listening to me, like I could teach him something. Until he heard me say I hadn't noticed Eve Gallagher. She was the girl from South Texas that came into the tool shop once a week to pick up one thing or other. She'd been fixing up the old three –story, her grandmother had left her. He'd been bugging me about dating again, but I wasn't interested. "Well, maybe she's not my type," I said. "Adam – man, you gotta be blind if you've never noticed that woman." "She's fine as all get out," Joseph poking and joking, coming down off the roof of the building. We'd been working that day on Mr. Saul's retail store across from our shop. We were just contractors. But we loved building things. I'd left the beautiful countryside of Wisconsin, to move to California and go into business with my best friend from college, Joseph Lents.

"I'm telling you Adam, she's got you in her cross

hairs." "I noticed her drooling the other day, when you came in out of the sun with your shirt off." Joseph was grinning like a pole-cat. "You did," I asked. "Of course man…she can't help it if she's got the HOTS' for you," he teased. "I admitted there were two reasons I hadn't dated yet since coming to Cali. One, I'd been too busy working and two, I didn't really know anyone. "You sly sleeper," said Joseph. "Have you ever heard the story of Adam and Eve?" "What are you talking about now," I asked. "You know… God put Adam to sleep and when he woke up there Eve was lying beside him." "Right, the air and elevation's making you a little woozy," I said. "Uh oh, what'd she forget this time," Joseph wiping the sweat from his upper lip with the back of his hand. I looked up for just a moment and I could have sworn there was a sparkle in her eyes. But then again, it could've been the sun's ray.

By the time I got down off the ladder, she was standing in the store's door way. "Hi, my names Eve," she smiled, holding out her hand for the shake. Joseph points his gun finger at me. Pretending to pull the trigger then disappears to the back of the shop. "Oh I'm sorry," I said. "Gotta excuse my partner, he's kind of…well anyway." "I'm Adam Washington," returning a cordial smile. "What can I do for you?" For the first time, I noticed her beauty and politeness. Standing there in her rustic blue jeans and old leather-worn cowgirl boots, with a tool belt wrapped around her waist. I could only imagine Joseph, in the chainsaw room preparing his speech - about Eve being my type.

I'd gotten lost somewhere between her hello and the hazel hues in her eyes. Before realizing she'd asked for help with the house she inherited. "So, what do you think?" "Can you help me?" "I've asked around town and they say you're one of the finest construction engineers." She said. "Yes, I'd love to Ms. Eve," my lips stammered…help you that is! " "Great!" she grinned. "What are your hours of availability?" "Well, we close here around four O'clock pm, if that's ok," I said. 'Joseph wasn't kidding,' I thought. Her wonderful- delightful personality was befitting to her beauty. "Then it's a deal – I mean you're hired," she said, with a funny little chuckle, interrupting my thoughts. "What other materials will you need?" I asked, blushing like crazy. I was starting to feel my fate had turned, while walking through the shop lightly chatting and picking out more nails and screws.

She was pretty funny, and I noted the crooked little smile that made her even cuter in some way.

"Adam," she said. All I heard was the way she called my name. "Your shops pretty cool," she finished. Afterwards, I wrapped up her tools. She paid the bill and stuck the sampler items in her tool belt. Walking towards the door, we stood on the sidewalk a bit longer. It seemed neither of us wanted to say good bye. Then she reached for my hand. I'd assumed for another handshake. Instead, she'd worked up enough nerve to invite me to enjoy some country stew. Sort of a thank you, she said, from her grandmother's old recipe she'd also inherited. I kindly accepted. Then inside, Joseph who seemed to have disappeared all together, reappeared. "What was that about," he asked. "Well buddy," putting my hand on his broad shoulder. "I guess my fate in a new town - has just changed." "And I reckon I've got you to thank for that." "I know - you're beaming," he said, taking my place behind the counter.

STORY THREE

LOVELY SHOES

"OH, GREAT, I TRIED TO NOT SOUND SO DESPERATE OR NERVOUS ABOUT SEEING HIM AGAIN."

I had spent the entire morning waiting on Boaz to show up at my store again. It was his dreamy eyes and well groomed attitude I'd fallen for. With much anxiousness, I'd been stuck in a funny daydream: the one where he comes into my store and I trip over my own feet trying to quickly get him the size shoe he requested. Then I get back to where he's sitting and he tells me it's the wrong color. "Hi Ruth," the voice said, bringing me back to myself. It was my co-worker; the beautiful tawny brown skinned Naomi. She was all out of breath. "Girl I just had to run all the way across the street." "Why?" "Ever been to the surplus store?" "No." "I had to go, to check for a certain pair of Stilettos' for the princess over there." "It's not polite to point," I said, looking at the woman checking out at the register. Naomi had been working at 'Snazzy-Snapping Shoes' for a while longer than me, but I'd come to appreciate her words of wisdom. "So how's your day been going," catching her breath? "You don't wanna know." "Wow…that bad huh?" "Well let's just say, I spent the first four hours in some kind of dream world." "I know. It's Mr. 'beautiful feet!" Naomi teased, scooting over in the isle to stock more shoes on the clearance rack. "You got me." I'd become somewhat worried, because the usual bi-weekly shoe browsing he'd done had stopped for some reason. "Ruth, don't worry, he'll pop up sooner or later." "Besides, he can't be done shopping yet," she joked. "He must have - what would you guess… about a hundred pair of snazzy shoes?" "Probably," I replied. "Wishing I could sell him a hundred more."

We finished stocking the clearance shoes and laughed our way through the day. Arriving home I tried to un-clutter my busy mind about Boaz. So I called another girlfriend up and asked if she'd like to meet me for caffeine-free drinks. Standing in line to

pay for the mochas, I rambled through my purse for cash. To find out I'd left my wallet home. And just when I'd given up all hope on what I thought was a crummy day; a sudden tap on the shoulder spent me around. "Excuse me miss, I'd like to pay for that if you'd let me." To my surprise, it was Boaz, the tall handsome gentleman, I'd dreamt about so often. Standing there with my mouth open and heart

pounding, "Boaz...Umm ....uh, yes," I mumbled my thanks. Oh god, I'd imagined stumbling over my feet in honor of serving him today - but stumbled my words instead. "I...I... haven't seen you in the store lately." "Yeah I missed you too, Ruth," giving me a dazzle of a smile. "I've been away on business for the last month." "Oh, great," I tried to not sound so desperate or nervous about seeing him again. "What brings you to this side of town," I asked. "Well I didn't have far to go." "I just live a few blocks away." "You do," I asked dumfounded. "Oh, excuse me Boaz; I want

you to meet my friend, Orpah." "Is that her in the corner?"

Orpah had been transfixed at the back table. To my surprise, she'd been watching Boaz from the time he walked into the little coffee diner. Need I say…I was elated he had come to my rescue? Lending his chiseled arm and escorting me to the booth where Orpah sat. "Hi, my names..." "Fancy Feet," Orpah finished his sentence. He then glanced at me and we all laughed. In the next few minutes, as I sat there sipping on my specialty coffee drink, I could feel there was something more between the two of us. "So I hear you're a traveling man," Orpah budded in between the silent trances between us. "Yes, I do quite a bit of that," he said, adding a pinch more creamer to his tall cup of chi tea. I'd never had a real chance before today to sit down and chat with him about who he really was and what he did. But that day,

as we sat a while longer my curiosities about him were pretty much resolved. He was an ambassadors' businessman. Who'd come into 'Snazzy-Snapping' to buy up shoes for several 'Ambassadors' in foreign countries. He'd then pack the shoes back to them because their jobs were too busy to tend to themselves. Well that was it for me. I was more impressed than ever with this charming chiseled shoe man. "That's great," I said. Just the thought of helping someone else shine forth in excellence for their country was extra special. "How about meeting next Friday?" "Wonderful," I smiled.

STORY FOUR

THE BUS RIDE

"ALL SHE WONDERED THE REST OF THE BUS RIDE, WAS... IF HE WAS MARRIED OR NOT."

Bobbi Dutcher checked her overflowing order before stepping onto bus number #2. Feeling a little excited about the business cards for the basket boutique she'd just opened. After paying her fare she surveyed a seat, dropping a handful of cards along the way. Stooping down to pick them up, the six-foot- two gentleman beat her to it. "Here you go," he said, flashing a cordial smile. She'd not been able to take her eyes off him for a moment. "Oh thanks," surprised he'd noticed. "May I," the man seemed interested in the type of business she was advertising. "It's a gift basket beauty treats store, Bobbi smiled back." "Well that sounds nice," he continued to read the business card. "Bobbi, Robbi and Shanti, which are you," he asked? Had she noticed a flicker of light-hearted-playfulness as the pleasant man's eyes connected with hers? Or was she just imagining things? From outer appearances, the dark haired man with the perfect groomed moustache had all the details her mother Shanti, had often spoken. As the kind of man she should date.

"I'm Bobbi," introducing herself pushing a card into his hand. "Well Bobbie I'm glad to have met you - thanks for the business card." "I'm sure it'll come in handy some time in my gift giving days." Both rising from the squatting position, the well-groomed gentleman offered Bobbi his open seat and then found another for himself. Just four rows ahead of her. He'd been riding the city bus at exactly 3:30p.m that day. Just as she was, both coming from downtown. The few words between them were quickly lived, as he reached up and pulled the buzzer for the Broadway street stop. Bobbie watched the cordial – polite man with the wonderful smile get off the bus with keys in hand, heading across the street into the park and ride lot, where he disappeared. And though he was gone like a whisper of breeze, all she wondered the rest of the bus ride, was… if he was married or not. And if so, could she maybe sell him a beautiful basket for his wife, sister or mother?

Arriving back at the boutique, she heard her sister's bossy voice yelling from underneath all the colored shredded basket fillers. Evidently, Bobbi had already received a call from a potential vendor wanting to help her establish an account for one of her product lines. This was all so new to Bobbi, opening a first time business. Robbi was Bobbi's right hand field rep and business partner. Not only was she smart and outgoing. But Bobbi had come to trust and appreciate Robbi, her twin sister's business savvy. Robbi was committed and determined to see the newly formed boutique take off and be successful. "Did you get his information?" "What," Robbi yelled back into the front of the shop. "Who was it," Bobbi asked? "Oh you've got an appointment with him on Wednesday of this week." "No way…." "Yes-way…what'd you think, I'd let him get a way," Robbi laughed out loud? "Did you get a name?" "He said…'he's pretty sure he can help us establish a few vendor accounts." "Plus he was the most funny business man I've ever spoken to." "I really think you ought to meet him and see if there's more than just business you can score." "Did you get a name?" "Yeah, it's Mr. Henderson."

Robbi had arranged for her sister Bobbi, to meet with the products vendor on the city's outskirts at 6:30p.m., Wednesday. Arriving in the little hick town, Bobbi double checked the address Robbi had given her. Thinking how mysterious a place it was.' Right at the edge of town where there was nothing much but old broken down railroad tracks and ancient story houses. As she drove around looking for the place she

noticed the street lighting was very poor and it seemed like a ghost town at night. "Who in the world would ever live way out here," she thought. "Oops, that must be it back there." She'd passed it up a few addresses shy. Backing up she swirled around on the empty road and went back to the funny looking hidden cove. Then getting out of the car she walked up the sidewalk and climbed the six porch steps. Using the old fashioned door knocker, she waited nervously. Did she really want to do this? She glanced down at the 'mini mouse' watch her sister had given her as a gift to celebrate their official store opening. She almost turned and left. When suddenly, she noticed standing in the doorway. "You again," she smiled, surprised but pleased. It was the fine tall gentleman she'd met on bus number two earlier in the week. "Come in," he smiled with a twinkle in his eye.

STORY FIVE

OPPOSITE ATTRACTIONS

"I'M DION GREEN." "FAITH," SHE REPLIED. HE HELD HER HAND LIKE HE WAS TRYING TO GET TO KNOW HER.

I'd been invited to a sand-castle competition at the Sandy Stone Beach, which was an annual event my son's elementary school held each summer. We'd gotten all the camping gear packed early enough to beat the rush hour traffic that Thursday. Till Bailey, suddenly came running out the house. He was our 'Chocolate Labrador. Reggie stroked the dog. "Mom, can we please take him." "I'm sorry son, not this time." Further down the road, my eleven- year-old son, became anxious to get there. Feeling a little pressured by his over-zealous nagging, I picked up speed just a bit. It was then that I almost collided into the dashing man in the dark green Subaru, getting off at the same exit as I was. "How dare he cross over the lane like that," Faith muddled under her breath. "He must be out of his mind," she kept thinking. After jumping off the freeway behind the man, Faith headed to the nearest gas station. To her surprise he came walking out of the little mini-mart with a 'Suzy Q'

cupcake in his hand. Looking Faith's way with a nod of the head and a big smile. Faith just looked at him with an uninteresting sneer.

After getting gas, the map read, the Oakley Stone Beach Cabins were less than five miles away. Reggie and I would be staying for just a few nights. "Let's see, taking a mental picture of her three day agenda." "Friday is sightseeing." "Then Saturday morning we'll meet the rest of the competing teams." "And by Sunday evening, it'll all be done and over with." Reaching their destination, Faith got unpacked, then headed for the nearest food vendor to get Reggie's favorite beach dog - foot long. "Oh my goodness, she thought…out of all the people who had showed up for the three days event, couldn't I have bumped into anybody else besides the crazy man?" "Hello, again." taking a big bite out of the 'foot-long' in his hand. After swallowing his food he continued. "I think we met abruptly…back at the gas station mini-mart." The man stared her down with what she thought was a ridiculous smile. "Yeah," she said slightly, keeping her real thoughts silent so as not to put her foot in her mouth, correcting the man on their meeting. "You mean you almost ran me over back there!" What was it about this guy that rubbed Faith the wrong way? She usually was a good judge of character. Or was she? She'd evidently, married the wrong fellow the first time, causing the walls and red-flags to flare up. But all she'd read about this man was his diverse personality - which was totally opposite of her ex-husband, Daniel. She'd run into this man three times now. And even though it was just "hi and bye," Faith had made up her mind to be nice to the guy. "I'm not letting down my walls," she muddled under her breath. "And I'm definitely going to stay out of his way." The evening rolled by and Reggie was sound asleep in the next room. Faith lay there on the front-room daybed wondering about the man who drove the dark green Subaru. She'd been so oblivious to him, while peeking over her tall heart walls; she'd no time to catch the man's name.

Glancing at the moons light piercing through the shades, Faith began to laugh out loud. She'd figured out the puzzlement. Not only was he opposite her ex, Daniel, but was also her opposite. She just giggled. After rising early Saturday morning and grabbing breakfast, everybody checked in with the competition team captains. "Could it be fate," Faith wondered, looking at the man walking towards her for the fourth meeting. "Excuse me," he said. "Fourth time's a charm eh," standing there in the white sand with one hand in his front jean pocket, holding the other out for a hand shake. "I'm Dion Green." "Faith," she replied. He held her hand like he was trying to get to know her. And she had to admit, the strong-firm squeeze felt rather good. Reminded her of the security she once felt a long time ago. As it turned out, He and I were put on opposite teams and ended up competing against each other in the castle building race. "So, you thought I was obnoxious at first?" "No I was just scared," Faith replied. "Of what," Dion asked curious? "I'm a divorcee and I didn't think I was ready to let my walls down." "And now," he smiled? "Now's Ok- I figured it out," she grinned ...chatting back and forth with Dion steadily pouring sand into the bucket. "Well, welcome to a converging friendship...you all right with that?" "Yeah, I think I'm ready to give love another chance."

STORY SIX

DEAR GOD

"I WAS HIDING THE FACT, I WAS REALLY APPREHENSIVE ABOUT ANOTHER RELATIONSHIP."

It all began with a prayer from 'a once shattered heart'. One day, when Eunice realized she'd been single for three years raising two sons on her own. She prayed, "Lord I'm tired of doing this all alone." "On top of that, I'm lonely." "Can you please find it in your list of things to do, to send me some help?" "Thank you!" A few months later I noticed the new VP of Security, who had graced our workplace. Rochelle, my co-worker, stepped in to play matchmaker. She'd planned to introduce us. Though I'd prayed sincerely, I was hiding the fact, I was really apprehensive about another relationship. After suffering the pain of a broken heart over a fifteen year marriage gone awry, I'd lost not only my home and possessions, but my confidence in finding security again, as well. "Now there's a man worthy of looking at." Rochelle had met me at the copy machine and pulled me aside early Tuesday morning. "What?" "He's a Vice-President…whew…he's got clout," she teased, leaning

up against the 20 pound paper box in the corner of the copy station. "Forget it!" "He has lots of money and I betcha… a big house to go with it." "Rochelle, are you crazy?" She just chuckled. Then grabbed her photocopies and headed towards the tall man in the pastel colored shirt that set off a pin-stripe tweed suit.

I managed to make it out of the corner in time to bypass their coming over. Later in the day during lunch break, Rochelle and I sat together strategizing how we'd meet the rest of the day's deadlines, with Tuesday morning meetings being such time – killers. I looked up and saw Vanessa Washington, another co-worker stepping out of the lunch line and flagged her down to join us at the table that seated four. No sooner had Vanessa sat down between the two of us, Rochelle moved over one seat and turned to wave at someone else entering the cafeteria. It was Tony, the new VP of Security. I was appalled. 'How obvious

could Rochelle get? - Apparently, pretty obvious. Rochelle directed Tony to the seat beside me, and then returned to her conversation with Vanessa. I decided I might as well be a good sport. So I got with the plan Rochelle had baited me into. "So, you're a Vice President?" I asked Tony. He had a dazzling smile and a sweet disposition as far as I could tell. And during our twenty minute casual conversation, between bits of food and silent swallowing, I found out he had a daughter, who was about to turn nine in two days. Well hearing that, sort of perked up my ears.

Here was someone that just maybe, I could relate to and have something in common with. His daughter, Crystal's turning nine would put her at exactly the same age as my middle son, Christopher. I could see that behind all the fancy dress and intellect, Tony was warm and very down to earth. And he certainly

wasn't shy letting on that he'd moved here for a fresh start with life and business. "So how do you like our mid-size town and larger than life company, so far?" "Well, as far as the town, my daughter says, I'm progressing at a normal pace." We both laughed looking up at each other in unison. "And, the weather, he continued....what can I say, there's no better weather anywhere." "You're right," I added my two-cents. "And the job, company...atmosphere... and surroundings," I went on?

Lunch had gone well that Tuesday afternoon. Eunice thought. But after arriving home, she rehearsed the day, thinking. "In her nervousness, of being left by her girl-friend-co-workers, alone with Tony, she was afraid the phishing for something else in common, she might've spoken a mouth full – too much! But this nice man had left Eunice, with the impression he'd not encountered anything so far, that

he didn't like. " And as she recalls…there was quite a few things about him, she did cherish. Like his "direct eye contact that at times held her attention. And his consistent smile, followed by a gala laugh. I do know one thing; personally, I hadn't felt that happy in years. Luckily, what I thought might end up in disaster that day at the lunch table, actually turned out to be one of the best lunches I'd ever sat down to, in the 'Zeroclund' cafeteria. We were a company of green technicians and consultants. Helping other companies reduce costs, by operating efficiently through environmental sustainability. Fortunately, Tony and I continued to meet for lunch for the next few months. Equally, each day we treasured getting to know one another a little more. Then, it dawned on me – "Oh dear god, you've answered my prayer!"

STORY SEVEN

A PILGRIMS' DINNER

"MY HEART FLUTTERED A BIT WHEN MAX ACCEPTED THE HOME COOKED MEAL THREE DAYS BEFORE THANKSGIVING."

Monday, November 21st. Exactly three days before Thanksgiving. Lucinda was standing over the kitchen sink cleaning the pie pans when she heard the sound of a diesel. Peeking through the pane, she noticed a slogan that read "Packed with Pride." The truck engine revved and then slowed to a stop, just across the road three houses down. It was the 'Mayflower Moving Company.' She turned off the water where she'd been rinsing. Stepping outside Lucinda watched the driver back the long truck into the open garage - where he jumped out of the front cab, stepped to the back and lifted the sliding door. Cupping her hands to her brow to block the sun, she slightly blushed at the handsome stranger. Busy setting lamps and chairs aside, before rolling down a brown-leather sofa on a dolly. "Afternoon neighbor," the man greeted with a big wave of the hand. "Good day." Lucinda responded, with a hint of surprise in her voice. "Hum," that house had been up for sale for

nearly six months now. Then here comes a dashing fellow and his family moving in. Five hours later, Lucinda realized the nice gentleman had been constantly at work since noon time. She figured it was time to be neighborly. So marching over to where the long truck was parked, she boldly introduced herself.

"Hi, I'm Lucinda Bibbens." She bolted out, standing in front of the chiseled man, who resembled a body builder. The man paused, and then charmingly said… "I'm Max Dutcher." "I'd been thinking about doing the same thing." He chuckled. It amazed her that they were both on the same page. "You were, um...I mean had been?" Right away, Lucinda noticed the natural chemistry between them. It was very nice and so was the sound of his voice, which was sort of gruff with a deep rich baritone sound. Lucinda liked that kind of a thing in a man – everything strong and capable.

"Yeah, I'd thought about being the neighborly one, but hadn't found that stopping point until now." He finished. "Well, I saw you'd been working non-stop and just wanted to welcome you and your family to the neighborhood before the evening grew late." Lucinda kept talking while glancing at the man's hands - surveying his vein-lines that traced up the middle of his forefinger all the way to his wrist. "Umm...no ring," her cheeks turned a rose color. "So why Carolina," she asked? "Well it's been on my radar for a while now." "Really, how's that?" "I promised my in-laws I'd move this way to be close." My wife, passed away of heart failure last year."

"Oh, I'm sorry to hear that." Lucinda felt embarrassed she'd pressed him into further conversation. "It's ok; I've healed well now." "That's great news." Lucinda couldn't help but notice the trace of large sweat beads that sat over Max's top lip.

Thinking... He must be starved by now. Whatever it was, she found it easy to talk to him – and just being near him brought a simple calm over her. "Max if it's not being too forward, I'd like to offer you some leftover dinner and peach cobbler." "That sounds scrumptiously-yummy," he laughed. "How about I dish that up for you and drop it off by the time you're finished here?" "It's a deal." Max was so grateful for the gesture; you'd have thought it was thanksgiving dinner or better.

My heart fluttered a bit when Max accepted the home cooked meal three days before thanksgiving. The next day, Lucinda dunked the pile of clean-dry-laundry on the coach, and then the doorbell rang. In hurried excitement, she opened the door to find Max Dutcher standing there. "Hi again," he said, pausing. "How's everything working at the house?" "Great," he replied, wringing his hands a little. "Uh…my in-laws have planned a thanksgiving dinner for the family,

and I was wondering if you'd like to go with me?" It was a mouth full, and I could tell Max was a bit nervous. But somehow, he'd managed to get it all out without fainting. After the delightful dinner, we arrived back at the house. Max opened my door and escorted me out. And I suggested an evening walk, where I'd tour him through the new neighborhood. "I wanna thank you for coming," He lifted Lucinda's hand, giving a kissing- peck on the back. Then he stepped off the porch. . Wow, did that just happen? For several years, Lucinda had been the only single-lady on her block. Then suddenly into her life pops a guy appearing like some pilgrim stepping off the 'May Flower' to settle in her town. For just a moment, she caught herself dreaming "Ohm... see you soon Max." "Yes you will," he said, softly whistling his way home.

STORY EIGHT

WANT AD LOVE

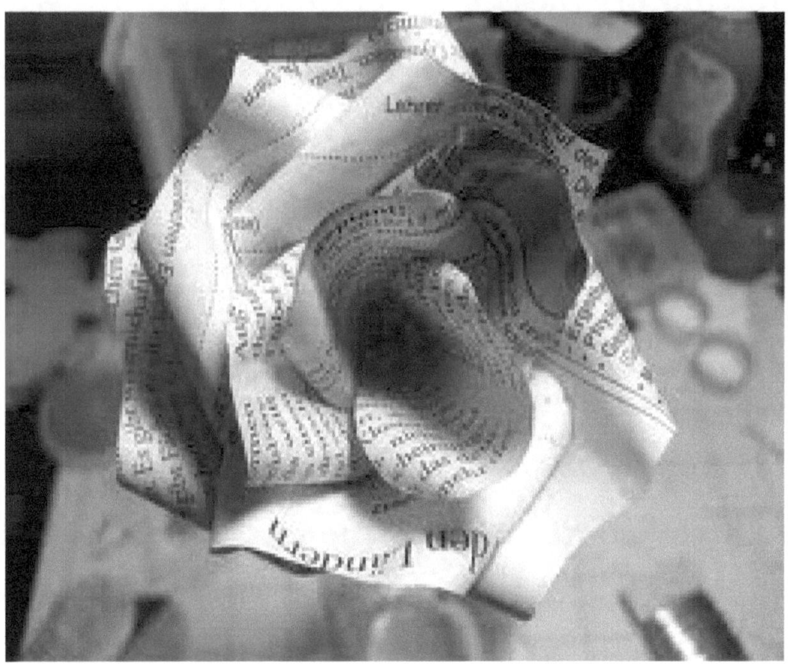

"HE WAS THE TALL HANDSOME SERVICEMAN SHE'D FALLEN IN LOVE WITH STRAIGHT OUT OF SENIOR HIGH."

"Earth to Gernie…this is Captain Catherine." My thoughts had been interrupted by my wonderful funny friend. "What's going on with you ... "Aren't you getting my messages," Catherine asked? "Why, did you call or email?" "Of course I did!" "Oh…thanks, but I'll be alright," I'd been stuffing my feelings back into the dark corner of my bruised heart. "Nope, it's not alright… I know you… something's bothering you….now spill it," she demanded! My friend knew me well, plus she had it right. This was the month of Charles and my 28th wedding anniversary, and I'd been a little emotional over the loss. Catherine had convinced me she had a sort of medicine that would make my woes better. So I'd gone ahead and placed the Ad like she suggested.

Early Sunday morning, Gernie sat at Joe's café' sipping a cup of tea and savoring a cake doughnut,

while thumbing through the Sunday Sentinel. She was looking for the singles section, where she'd placed an Ad and wanted to see if it met her satisfaction. "Oh there it is," she said, skimming through the short paragraph which read: "Trustworthy white female, 45, 5' 4, 135 pounds, blonde hair, green eyes, clean life, in great shape, love kids, outdoor events and camping. Crazy about Ruthless and Gracious, my dogs, good sense of humor, affectionate, quiet times at home, seeks honest, long term relationship of the opposite sex, please contact Gernie at 555-9119." She hadn't dated, since Charles; her husband had been declared dead after he'd gone missing from a military mission. She was very impressed with the layout of the Ad and so she finished her tea, said good day to Mr. Graham, and happily left.

On the drive home, Gernie's mind drifted back to

the lovely romantic times she'd shared with her wonderful Charles. Picturing the smile that made her feel she could conquer anything - except losing him. He was the tall handsome serviceman she'd fallen in love with straight out of senior high. The man she cherished dearly. The way he suited up in his captain blues and proposed to her under the American flag standing on the college football field. The date was drawing closer and Gernie imagined… him like it was yesterday. The thoughts were so strong she could almost smell the 'Classic-Cool-Cologne,' he'd worn. Snapping out of it she brought herself back to the present.

Several weeks had passed and the other employees were curious about Gernie's bubbling-blushes and happy feelings around the office. "You sure are a radiant ray these days…what's gotten into you," Catherine laughed. "Come on…out with it," she kept

coercing. I'd lost focus wondering if my savvy fashion designer could whip together an outfit for my dinner-date in two days. "So, what is it," Catherine nudged again, breaking my concentration? "It's a date!" "What, you're kidding me." "No kidding…remember the 'single-man-wanted Ad?" "Yes." "I finally got a call after three weeks." "Who is he," "I don't know yet..." I'm meeting him for the first time, day after tomorrow." "Meeting who for the first time," Hillary, another close co-worker budded in. "She's got a date," Catherine whispered. "Supper… where you guys going," Hillary wanted more? "You'll never guess…out of all the places in town, he picked a spot dear to my heart." "He suggested the Golden Metropolis Restaurant." "Wait a minute… didn't that used to be…uh...you…" "Me and Charles favorite place, it most certainly was." I was so excited that afternoon; I had finished Catherine's sentence. I wasn't sure what fate held for me, but whatever was

happening it sure seemed like all the old memories of love had been refreshed since I placed that 'AD.'

At 5p.m., Catherine put the finishing touché to Gernie's dress. She'd designed this one especially for her friend in hopes of her finding love again. Arriving at Metropolis, the greeter welcomed Gernie. "Can I help you?" "Reservations for Kirkwood," she said. "Oh right…Mrs. Kirkwood… Mr. Kirkwood's waiting for you at table seven. Did I hear right, a man with my last name, Gernie stood startled for a moment with her mouth opened wondering what a coincident? The greeter led her to the elegantly dressed table, where sat a man with his back to her, overlooking the calm and cloudy green water. His build was perfect from what she could notice under the dim lighting. His hair appeared light brown entwined with silver gray strands. Suddenly, Gernie's emotions ran haywire, and her eyes filled with tears, when the extinguished

gentleman stood up and turned around. "Charles, she cried, I prayed it would be you." "Yes Gernie, it's me," the gentle voice replied. Charles face broke into a huge smile as he reached for my hand pulled me in close and kissed me. Gernie sighed. His hug felt incredible.

STORY NINE

SPIRIT OF LOVE

"NOT ONLY WAS ANTONIO MARTIN, SMITTEN WITH HER WITTY-BEAUTY, BUT HE'D HAD A CRUSH ON JANELLE, EVERY SINCE SHE SAVED HIS COUSIN RICKY FROM DYING."

Are you sure you're going to be okay, Gail asked? With a slight nod of head and a fixed smile, Janelle said, of course, I just thank you for coming with us tonight. Sure not a problem, Gail responded. Then reaching over, she grabbed her friend around the neck and hugged her. She thought about how sad this time of year must be for her best friend. You know, Janelle said, I couldn't have done this alone. You weren't alone, your grandparents were here. I know, but you know what I mean. They're great and all, but sometimes I feel like I can't talk to them, like I can with you. I get it, Gail Responded. Don't think about it, besides what are good friends for, huh. Gail nudged Janelle with a playful and light attitude. She'd been trying to take her mind off the memory of what tonight's dinner represented.

It was December again and Christmas Eve already. But for Janelle Norton, it had rolled around too fast. Gail Shimmer had stood outside the Geronimo Restaurant on Canyon Road, trying to be a support, just as she'd done for the last three years. Janelle's routine had been the same. Just like clockwork. The single and beautiful twenty seven year old doctor had arranged a flight for her grandparents, out to Santa Fe, New Mexico, where they'd sit in silence, while Janelle reminisced over the loss of her parents. This happened every Christmas Eve. This family meeting and dinner wasn't just a celebration for Janelle's birthday, but unfortunately, it also marked the memorial of her parent's death, which had died in a plane crash while headed to France to celebrate their 30th wedding anniversary.

Arriving home that night, Janelle thought about how hard it had been moving forward with her life. And although that was true, it seemed she still was stuck with the haunting memories. The next day the phone rang. Hello, Janelle answered, it was a work buddy from the Christus St. Vincent Medical Center, where she worked. Hey Antonio, how are you. I'm just great beautiful, I was worried about you. I hadn't heard from you since you left for your holiday vacation. Is everything alright? Yeah, I think so. Not only was Antonio Martin, smitten with her witty-beauty, but he'd had a crush on Janelle, every since she saved his cousin Ricky from dying. He'd been shot five times in a tragic drive-by shooting initiation. Antonio and Ricky has been grateful every since. Hey, uh…I was calling, because a bunch of us from the hospital are taking off early tomorrow to go serve holiday lunches to the homeless, over in the northern community. And we'd love to have you

come. So what do you say…would you join us? He waited for the silence to break on the other end of the phone. Janelle's mind had escaped to another time and place as she stood there with the phone in hand, shocked at the invite. It was just what she'd needed to shake her out of the stupor she'd been in. And for the last three years, she'd never thought about anyone else but herself. And the pity party she'd been having all alone. Always blaming the job's busy schedule and lack of sleep for the reason she'd stopped mingling with friends.

"Janelle!"Antonio brought her back to the present. "Are you still there?" "Oh yes...yes, ah…that sounds wonderful, what time?" "Twelve noon," he replied. "Ok. How should I do this…you meet me here… or I come,"…she hesitated. "Oh, yeah… right!" Antonio, had been breathing hard himself, on the other side of

the receiver. "So...I'll pick you up around noon," he said. "Oh...and Janelle, wear your cute little Santa – Hat, the purple one." "Now how did he know about that," she wondered. Purple was her favorite color, and she'd had a special purple Santa cap for years. But she'd never worn it to work. "Alright, see you tomorrow," she said, then hung up the phone.

After returning to her bedroom, Janelle crawled up into bed and curled up her knees with a crumpled pillow. The old Purple Santa Hat stirred up more memories. Taking her mind way back, to the times when she was a little girl, when she, mom and dad used to go out into the neighborhood delivering Christmas gifts to poor single moms who'd lost their husbands to the wars. Or some wives had even been abandoned and left with a house full of children, due to divorce. This was the spirit of love she remembered and had no idea she'd missed.

Since her parent's death, Janelle had sort of started her own tradition and forgot about the good deeds her parents had done during the holiday seasons. She thought about how much fun they'd had together. And what spirit of joy she'd experienced back then. "It was a great feeling," she recalled - "Making someone else feel good." Equally, she was grateful for Antonio's call tonight. Tomorrow would be Christmas day and she needed this outlet just as much as those hungry people needed her and the hospital crew. After the evening was over she realized she'd been blessed beyond measure. She was already putting together a plan for next year. She'd do something altogether different. So Janelle decided to spend a portion of her inheritance to open up her own Christmas Eve feeding center. She felt good about dedicating the center as a memorial to her folks. And

as planned, the next year, just a week before Christmas, she flew the grandparents out to help volunteer with the effort. It was her way of keeping the spirit of love alive.

STORY TEN

SWEET LOVE

"BUT THE THOUGHT OF A MAN THAT HAD BAKING SKILLS SENT COZY WARMTH UP HER BONES."

Hanna had been dying for the long awaited trip to the smoky mountains. It was all she'd thought about for the last few weeks. How she'd step back into time, enjoying the serenity of quietness, where she'd ease her cares away with a warm wood burning fire. Or maybe she'd sit relaxing in an old porch rocker while gazing those mountains. Well that's what she'd started dreaming up anyway. But then, she snapped back to reality. Besides the Appalachian cabins being tucked securely away, she probably wouldn't really get the quietness she'd hoped for - since she was sharing a log cabin with friends. Nevertheless, the weekend getaway would give her a break from the hectic week and complex work load she'd carried. So taking off a bit early on Friday, Arleta, a friend from work, gave her a ride home. "Thanks for the ride," Hanna waved goodbye. Arleta smiled, blew the horn, and drove away.

It was exactly 2:00pm when Hanna stepped through the front door and the phone rang. "Hello, this is Hanna." "Oh Miss Robinson, how are you?" "I'm fine, who's this." "It's Fileapae, from the garage of Town and Country Cars." "Oh hey, Fileapae what's up?" "I called to let you know your Jeeps ready." "Great, so it's ready?" "Yes." "When can I pick it up?" "Anytime from now till closing at 8:00pm," he replied. "Wonderful, I'm on my way." "Give me about thirty minutes or so, and I'll be there." Hanna stuffed the rest of her things into the suitcase and then called a cab. Arriving at the Town & Country dealership, she hung out in the waiting area. A few minutes later, a man stepped forward making a funny sound. He'd been clearing his throat for some odd reason, when Hanna looked up from the magazine she'd been thumbing through. Standing to her feet she looked the man in the eye and introduced herself. "I'm Hanna

Robinson." "I'm here to pick up my Jeep." "I was told it was ready." Hanna's gentle but stern voice left the man standing in front of her, at a loss for words … "Uh yeah… about the jeep." "The front wheels still need to be rotated. And the GPS needs adjusting." "But, I was told it was ready," Hanna sounded a little frustrated. "I'm sorry but it's not quite there yet. Like I said, once those things are done you'll be as good as new." Hanna couldn't keep the mad fuss up with the nice gentleman dressed in the oily mechanics suit. He'd been cordial beyond measure, and mostly listened with his eyes. The silence pierced the air for just a moment, and then the man turned and introduced himself as Nick. "Thank you for sticking around so we can make sure you're safe in your travels." "No, thank you Nick, I appreciate it," she said.

"I apologize for my assistant worker, Fileapae.

He's fairly new and had no business telling you the vehicle was ready. I take full responsibility for the mistake." But Hanna understood and overlooked the misunderstanding. If anybody knew about work complexities, she did. "Would you like some fresh coffee?" "I'd love some." The man moved to the instant coffee bar, where he proceeded to wait on her, by pouring some coffee into the disposable cup. He'd noticed her big wide green eyes. They seemed to sparkle up against the green collar of the silk blouse she had on. "Sugar," he asked? "Yes…, five packets please." Nick looked up again marveling her beauty. "If you don't mind my asking, how'd you get here so quickly?" "I rode a cab, and it seemed like he'd taken flying lessons from somewhere," she joked. Nick laughed. Thinking how he admired a woman of beauty and laughter. "I see you like sweets also," he said. "Huh?" she looked puzzled at first; he'd caught her off guard. "Sweets," he repeated. "You asked for five sugars." "I love sweets," she smiled. "That's a nice change, he said. "I was thinking Hanna; maybe I could have you over to the cake shop sometime." "You bake cakes?" "Yes, I do that in my spare time - when I'm not here."

"Usually its sugar or grease," he'd begin to tease back a bit. The conversation with Nick wasn't only polite and comfortable for Hanna, but it put her at ease about driving the jeep up the snowy mountains by herself. "Excuse me," I'll check on your vehicle to see how much longer." After Nick stepped away to the back of the building, Hanna sat smiling about his friendly – polite and funny demeanor. She especially loved his customer service skills. But the thought of a man that had baking skills, sent cozy warmth up her bones. It was because she remembered how her dad used to bake pies for every special occasion her family had. Like every birthday, anniversary, thanksgiving

and even Christmas. Her dad baked homemade pies. It was like he'd been blessed with some kind of sweet love. And boy did her mother love it. It made their relationship even sweeter, to see her dad do such a thing. "How sweet is this", she thought …a man who's into sweets probably as much as I am."

Hanna had decided in her mind already. "If he asks me out, I'm accepting." A tiny smile creased her mouth. 'Oops, sorry did I scare you?" Nick had slipped back from the garage, into the sitting area again. "No- not scare-just startled me." He'd touched her on the shoulder and it was like an electric shock sent chills through her body. "Hey, before I get you checked out of here, can I invite you to some coffee and dessert," he asked. "Why of course," she replied. Then reaching into her purse to grab a business card, she handed it to Nick. My numbers right there, pointing to a phone number under the writing that

read...'Gourmet Muffins & Designer Coffees.' She couldn't help but observe the smile on his face the whole time he read the business card. "What's that grin," she asked. "Nothing," he hid what he'd wanted to say...for the moment. "Did I overhear you say you were leaving town in the morning?" "Why, were you listening to my phone conversation earlier?" "Yeah, I'm guilty," he confessed, smiling. "I'm headed to the mountain to meet some long time friends of mine and we're spending the weekend up there." "Wow, I guess you're in for some sweet pleasurable surprises this weekend," Nick said. Hanna had missed the tiny clue as to why Nick had been grinning so hard. He'd been trying to hide a secret from Hanna, she had no idea about. "You know you're not only funny, but you're interesting," she said, blushing. Her intuition had already told her, Nick would make a great friend, but what she didn't know was that her other friends Jackie, Drake, Billy and Rhoda, had something to do

with her meeting Nick today.

So, the next day, early Saturday morning, before the sunrise, Hanna was ready to hit the road. Nick and the guys at the dealer's garage had fixed her jeep, rotated the tires and chained them up for her. She now felt safe and calm for the drive up to the mountain. Indeed, it had been an easy drive. Now the escape from the hustle and bustle of modern times awaited her. Driving alone she observed the old unique shopping stores, museums and golf ranges, while exploring the array of wildflowers that blossomed the fields. After driving about 100 miles the GPS automated voice system, interrupted… "Ten miles to Wild Mountain Cabins," the lady with the quirky voice said. When Hanna finally arrived, Drake and Billy stood on the old oak porch grinning, while the girls, Jackie and Rhoda, headed her off at the path, where they met her at the car with a homemade

basket full of sweet cinnamon – chip muffins. "Wow – what's this…guys," she asked. "Yum…these smell wonderful and I'm famished from the long drive." She pinched off a muffin and put a piece in her mouth. "Man that's almost as good as daddy's pies," she said. "Who made these?" Just then, Nick stepped out onto the cabin porch with a hunter-green apron on. "Guys ….what are you four up to," she asked? Nick just stood there waving. And Hanna, well this was a sweet surprise as she too stood there grinning back.

STORY ELEVEN

RAINY ROMANCE

"IT HAD BEEN HIS RADIATING GOOD CHRISTIAN HUMOR THAT BRIGHTENED HER DAY — DESPITE THE RAINY WEATHER OUTSIDE AND THE CLOUD THAT HAD HUNG OVER HER HEAD."

It was the middle of October and the raindrops pelted the water's surface in the Sacramento Valley. That was where 38 year old Lexis O'Donnell lived. Instead of a sense of calm and quiet, the recent brewing rain storms had left Lexis in a state of gloominess. It reminded her of all the changes in her life she'd encountered lately. And though for Lexis, the rain at times made her feel peaceful; it was at this moment, that it reminded her of a powerful destructive source. As her mind went back to the day she'd received the long distance phone call! Indeed, it was the one that conjured up all the depression and sadness she'd felt. "No!" Lexis heard herself say over the phone. "That can't be right!" "I'm sorry to have to be the one to call with such bad news," said Mr. Stewart. "But our hearts are broken also." "We just wanted you to know because you two were best friends forever." "Plus you, Lexis, are just like a

daughter to us." "Thank you Mr. Stewart," Lexis said. "I appreciate it….but I don't know if I'll be able to come to the services – and I will keep you in my prayers." "Thank you He said." "Now remember, you can call us in a few days, if anything changes with your decision to come," Mr. Stewart encouraged. "We should have all things ready for the funeral by Thursday of next week." "Ok, I will…love you too"… and she hung up the phone.

Roaming through the house towards her bedroom, Lexis flopped down on the bed and belted out sorrowful tears. She couldn't believe it. Such a young woman, cut down in the prime of her life by a gruesome deadly disease such as cancer. She hated the thought of losing her best friend. And all she wanted to do right then was die herself, at the pain she'd felt and the unforgiveness she'd not let go of. So Lexis decided to do her best to get through this. So she chose to deal with it momentarily, her way – by pulling the pain of her friend's death up front and personal, while pushing the thought of forgiveness way to the back of her mind. The day rolled by and it was now 6:00pm. Restless, she wondered back and forth between the living room and bedroom. Where she continued to blow her nose and wipe the tears. Later, sitting in the middle of the queen size sleep comfort bed, Lexis pried the top off the hat box, where she'd kept the old Kodak-camera pictures for what seemed like eons ago. Following, she looked at them with childhood reminiscence. Crying and constantly tossing wadded up tissues to the side of the ruffled ivory blanket, she held up another picture of Shipley Rae Stewart, rubbing her fingers across the one 5 x 7 glossy print!

Lexis and Shipley had been blood sisters since second grade. She'd recalled the act that day in the

neighborhood of College Park, Illinois - where they'd both grown up as native residents. It was a hot summer's eve in July, when the girls ran out to the back yard of Shipley's parent's home. That's when it happened – their bonding friendship tie. And now, it appeared so real that she almost heard Shipley's laughing. Yet still the memories caused more heart pain. It was a pact where the girls had evidently determined to be sisters for life – a surreal scene of both girls puncturing their fingers. She could almost feel the tinge of the needle's pinch. A needle Lexis had snuck from her mother's sewing kit that same afternoon. "We never fought or disagreed about anything, she muttered under her breath – a tiny smile creased her mouth. In contrast, fond memories abruptly turned bitter at the next photo which popped up. It was Charlie Stewart, Shipley's older brother. The two of them Lexis and Charlie, were making goofy faces huddled together under the old

apple tree in Charlie's front yard. The picture was a deceiver. While Lexis viewed him as a friend, Charlie had other ideas. Unfortunately, theirs was a friendship gone wrong. She licked the salty tear drop that rolled down her left cheek. She'd regretted the sordid incident of the past, which had held up her blessing to forgive.

"Hi Lexis," Charlie said, standing in the doorway. "What's up," she asked? "Noting much, I was getting ready to go visit a friend of mine," he said. "Sounds like fun - is Shipley here?" "No but she'll be right back." "Really," Lexis asked? "For sure…she just went down to the corner market to buy a quart of milk." "You can wait inside if you like," Charlie had lied. It was that day that Lexis had decided to keep the secret of the horrible altercation between him and her. It had been 21 years now, but she never forgot what Charlie had said. Neither had she been able to find a way to forgive him for the improper treatment towards her. It was this hidden poison which drove her away to another place, forcing her to reside in another city away from her best friend, Shipley. Several months had passed, and Lexis never did call Mr. and Mrs. Stewart back. Nor did she attend the funeral services of her best friend. She recognized the heartache of Shipley's death was enough. She didn't ever want to reopen the can of worms that had rotted away years ago. Nevertheless, the crying spells were over and she'd gotten through her grieving. So she decided to revisit the hat box. It was there she'd run across an old unfinished transcript. In her mind she'd seen herself dusting it off again and going back to college to finish her degree in ministry. She had an earnest desire to minister and work with young women who may have experienced what she had during the altercation with her best friend's brother, Charlie.

Putting the past behind, it was late October. And Lexis loved the smell of autumn in beautiful Sacramento Valley, where leaves glistened with splashes of raindrops, offset by bright green foliage. This was her favorite time of year. She'd grown accustom to the mild to cool wet rains, that left temperatures around the mid-40s F to low-50s F. But this morning Lexis stood on the sidewalk waiting at the light to cross the college campus. When suddenly, an inconsiderate driver out of nowhere, sped by and splashed a puddle of muddy water all over her. "Hey," the male voice called out at her from across the road. Lexis drew her focus away from the wet muddy mess that had landed all over her coat, onto the attention of the man heading towards her. The stranger looked a little frantic, as he stood facing Lexis, all out of breath. "I'm Malcolm," he said. Silently she looked with wonderment at the man with the dishwater-blonde

hair and concerned blue eyes. Then brushing the water from her coat she introduced herself. "Hi…uh…, Lexis," she smiled. Then the man reached into the pocket of his grey trench-rain-coat and handed her a dry handkerchief. "Thank you!" She'd been a little embarrassed at how she looked, as she took the hanky. Then tucking her wet hair behind her ears, she asked. "Did you see that? " "Yeah, sorry to say I did." "It was like he did it on purpose." "I know, how weird." She said with a disheartened sound of voice. "You go to 'Capital,' "he asked? "Yes, I just started back," she said. Lexis admired the man's politeness, as he continued to walk and talk with her. "You might not recall but I was here two years ago," he said. "You were," she replied. "Yes, I was in fact." "What did you major in?" "World Evangelism," he commented. His smile was perky and warm. "And now," Lexis asked with interest? "Well, now I'm finishing my doctorate in Church Theology." "That's

wonderful," she ended her speaking. Then they both continued to skip over large puddles of water.

Lexis surprised herself with the gentleman that morning. It was a refreshing change from what she had been through. It was as if the misty rain was like some kind of renewal of joy that had crept back into her life. He didn't seem to mind the muddy water all over her light tan trench coat. Or that her big locks of curls had fallen out. So she lavished herself in his cordial concern. Then arriving at the front door of Capital Bible College, his eyes linked with hers and she felt butterfly flutters in the pit of her stomach, when he opened the door. "Thank you," Lexis smiled. Then she took a right turn and headed for class. "Wait….do you get a lunch today?" … Malcolm's voice followed her down the hallway. "Yes, 1:30pm…school cafeteria, be there," she replied back. Later sitting in the classroom her mind wondered at the magic of

Malcolm's appearing. "It had been his radiating good Christian humor that brightened her day – despite the rainy weather outside and the cloud that had hung over her head several weeks ago.

STORY TWELVE

SPARKLING HEARTS

"ANDREW CROSS, HAD DONE EVERYTHING WITHIN HIS POWER TO FIND THE PERFECT GIFT FOR THE LOVE OF HIS LIFE, VANDIAA.

It was the middle of a hot July summer when Andrew Cross got called away to a tour of duty with the United States Marine Unit. All Vandiaa could think about was the lonely days and nights she'd have to spend by herself before it was all over. What would she do with herself for the next eight months? She wondered. "You're going to be ok? Andrew said, kissing her goodbye. They'd both been standing in the driveway of the military housing unit, where they'd unpacked their things just days earlier. Vandiaa thought about how quickly the last two years had gone for her husband Andrew and her. Let's see, first boot camp training, then all the ins and outs of military procedure and protocol. They both had talked about how they'd felt and even what they'd do when the time did come. But that wasn't a reality now that the time was really here. In fact, they still weren't ready for this big surprising day of

deployment, especially since they'd only been at their duty station for less than a year.
"I love you." "You know that don't you?" "Yes I do… wonderful man," she laughed. Vandiaa kissed her husband back and hugged him even tighter. Then she released his hand. "Jack, you take care of him for me." She'd asked her friend's husband to watch over her man, Andrew, since they were being deployed together. Vandiaa felt a little better after they pulled off and she'd gone in the house to pop a can of Dr. Pepper. But quickly after drinking it, she ran to the restroom to throw it up. She thought maybe she had a weak and upset stomach due to all the nervousness of Andrew's leaving.

"Wrap-a–Tap-tap, "came the knock on the wooden screen door which sat midway off the sliding track, allowing the flies freedom to squeeze in. it appeared the secluded base housing units needed a lot of

maintenance and care. For a moment the ugly thought that crept up tried to take Vandiaa captive. 'That living conditions as an army wife wasn't quite her cup of tea.' Vandiaa had thought about what she'd envisioned as a little girl. In deed she'd dreamt of marrying someone more prominent. Like maybe a doctor, lawyer or even an ambassador of some foreign country. It was crazy for her to bring this up now that Andrew was gone and she knew it was just a passing thought. It must've been the early bouts of loneliness. The thoughts soon passed as she chuckled at her own foolishness, wondering how she'd even let it get the best of her. Snapping out of her negative zone, Vandiaa yelled from the bathroom where she'd gone once again to get a cold towel for her face. "Come in!" "It's me, Tully, the voice came echoing back. "Wanna got get some beer down at the club?" "No," Vandiaa said walking out with a cold towel on her forehead. "Oh my goodness, what's wrong?" "Nothing much, I

was just washing my face." "You look flushed." "You sure you're ok?" "Yeah, I think I was just overly nervous about Andrew's first deployment." "Well it'll be fine." "He's with Jack...Right?" "I guess," Vandiaa said! Tully, gave her a little hug and turned towards the door. "Looks like it's…no partying for you tonight huh?" "Nope, I'm gonna stay here and turn in early." "Ok, I'll check on you when I get back from Melton's Bar Hop." "Thanks," Vandiaa said, and then closed the front door.

I had been observing all the changes I'd not been used to, while on the military base. My husband's first deployment would only last eight months at the most, but to me that was a long time. That night that Tully left the little duplex housing unit, Vandiaa laid in bed thinking what she'd do to keep busy and out of trouble while her husband was away. So the next day she went out and applied for several jobs. One at the small library and resource center, the other at the military base store, and luckily she landed the one at the canteen. As the days went by, Vandiaa had begum to notice all the other wives playing at the playground with their children. She began to long for Andrew's company. Then her mind ran through the park with the little ones. Thinking how nice it would be to have a family, while she was still young. She'd be turning 30 years old on February 14th, so this was the year she'd wanted to get busy with this agenda of child bearing. Yeah, in the past she'd imagined what her life would've been like if she would have married that doctor or lawyer.

"Eh...probably would've been way more boring than this," she muttered under her breath. Smiling at the lady who'd stood in front of her at the cash register.

"Hi Sue, how are you today?" "Fine, thank you, Sue replied. "How's little Ricky and Desiree?" "They're great!" "They are at day care today, which helps me to get this shopping done." "I see. ….well you enjoy the rest of your evening," Vandiaa said, sending Sue on her way with a basket full of food and clothing. The commissary was a place everyone loved to spend a lot of time at, especially, if you had kids. The prices were beyond fair and well there were just too many cute clothes and things to fondle over for kids.

After Vandiaa arrived home from work, her feet were drastically swollen. Stepping out of a warm bubble bath she laid in bed with her legs and feet propped up on a pillow. "This should take care of that swelling," she kept speaking with herself. Then she heard the laptop email buzzer alarm. She knew it was Andrew. Pulling up the webcam she smiled from ear to ear to get to talk to her man again. "Hey baby, I miss you." "I miss you too honey." "How's everything back there?" "It's fine." "I got a job." "You did?" "Yes, it's working the cash register at the commissary."

"Well I'm proud of you honey." "Me too," she said "It's only been a few weeks and it seems like months already." "I don't know if I can do this." The tears welled up in her eyes. "Take it easy – you can do this - you're strong." "Am I?" "You betcha, you're the strongest woman I know, that's why I married you," Andrew consoled her. "Ok, if you say so," she said…feeling a bit better. That night after their little talk, Vandiaa decided to put her mind to good use. She'd make a list of things she wanted to accomplish in the next 8 months while Andrew, her husband was away on duty.

She thought she'd start with a little outreach; by gathering with a group of women who were in the same boat as she was… 'Feeling lonely since their husbands had gone to serve their country.' So the very next day Vandiaa started her bucket list of things to do. Sitting in the library that day she jotted down on the tablet a list of things which stated she'd Start a women's espresso-table-talk-team –meeting once a month at her home. Throw a birthday party once a month for one of the neighborhood kids. Read at least two good romance books before Andrew returned home. Volunteer one off day a month to help stock the shelves at the base's elementary school. Get her exercise regime back. Be a pen-pal to Andrew's unit – by sending encouraging cards. Pray for her husband's unit everyday for the next 8 months. "There she said out loud sitting in the middle of the bed. Vandiaa had finished bucket list of things she wanted to target in the next eight months. She felt rather good about what she'd determined to do.

Eight months had flown by and today was not only a big day, but it was Valentine's Day. Equally, Andrew Cross would be returning home from Iraq and Vandiaa would be turning 30 years old. So she sat anxiously on the couch with her feet propped a top the coffee table, waiting to hear that vehicle's horn blow. But drifting off into the days gone by, Vandiaa felt she'd learned so much in such a short time. Not only had she held down a nice job, that afforded her to make her home a pleasant place for her returning hubby, but she'd finished a list of appraising things she'd set her mind too. The only regret she'd had was the sad unfortunate of losing a friend. Tully had had fallen out with her. So Vandiaa had to cut all ties. It was due to the fact that Vandiaa had been clued into the secret of Tully's cheating on her husband, Jack. It just made everyone around there sick. Her going down to Melton's Bar Hop had gotten out of hand.

When Vandiaa tried to intervene as a friend, Tully bit her head off and it was this type of behavior that had caused an appreciation inside of Vandiaa. A gratefulness that she'd kept busy in a positive way

and stayed true to her husband. Vandiaa realized also through the long absence of her husband Andrew, that she had a great lover and a wonderful relationship with him. She was fonder of him now than then and she respected him dearly. But she never bad-mouthed Tully. And neither would she be the one telling Jack. She chalked it up as 'flaws' that all good people can get tangled up in at times. Meanwhile, just days earlier, "Andrew had done everything within his power to find the perfect gift for the love of his life, Vandiaa, his wife. And now this evening they stood in the middle of the military banquet room where he danced with her, marveling her radiance on her thirtieth birthday. "You look lovely," he said, then gave her a gentle spin around the floor. "Man this is sure a great surprise for me." His energy level was high. "Do you know you're my hero?" "Really," she smiled. "Most certainly so," he added, putting his hand on her big balloon belly. You

see not only had he searched out the perfect gift for her birthday, before returning home, But Vandiaa kept her pregnancy a surprise - secret just for his returning. "I Love you," they sang to each other as the song ended. It was like some kind of sparkling of hearts that evening for the two of them.

STORY THIRTEEN

LOVES SHINY KNIGHT

"Elliot was pretty crazy about Emma. Not only was she good for him, but she had the same goals & values."

Intro:

Emma Oliver sat in the cab smiling, when she remembered the conversation she'd had with her girlfriend "Radius." She'd mentioned to Radius that she'd almost given up on men. That was until she met her newest bow, Elliott Jenkins. It was a cold winter night when she ran out of the office building and jumped into the right side of the cab and he the left.

Emma and Radius:

The two women had sat that afternoon in the coffee bar sipping fat-free cappuccinos. When Emma, mentioned how tired of dating she was. Especially, since she'd been doing it for several months now. Like some kind of workout routine regimen, that was tied to her life. "You know I've been on so many blind dates I'm worn out." Emma said to Radius. "I understand you're tired, but don't give up just yet." "These things do take some time." I know for sure that when you've been out of the dating game for so long it can be kind of taxing." Radius tried to make her feel a bit more encouraged with the dating scene. "My problem is I've not found anyone that meets my standards yet." "I'm beginning to wonder if there are any legitimate Christian single men in my category." Emma went on with the yapping and yawning. "Is it that your drink has no caffeine in it? Or is it that all this dating talks' boring you to sleep?" Radius slightly chuckled. "I think it's both." "Well how do really feel," asked Radius? "Are you going to give up so soon?" "Ah...maybe I'll give it a rest and check back in a few months," Emma replied. "Besides, all I can think about is what my grandmother used to say – back in the day." "What was that?" "Oh she used to tease about couples finding the right top to match their type of pot." "Grandma would say…dating was just like

cooking." Well that's kind of cute." Radius continued to look at her friend wide eyed and open eared. "Yeah, granny was really something."

A sigh of pleasant relief left Emma's voice as she spoke about her Grandma Shirley. "I recall gram saying... "'There's always a lot of prepping for homemade soup - before the stewing and enjoying.'" "Wow, never heard it put that way – about love," Radius smiled. "Then again, Gram was a little eccentric." "Want to know something else?" "What else?" Her friend paid close attention. "Funny that the guys I've managed to drag myself out for, a lunch here...a dinner there." "None of them seem to get me." "I mean...there's been no chemistry or anything in common." It was now 1:45pm. The women had sat and talked for about an hour and a half now. Emma Oliver had begun to sound like a scratched record in

the ears of her friend Radius Copeland. But she just kept smiling and somewhat agreeing. "Is it really that hard to find a good guy who wants to date a 45 year old voluptuous woman?" They both burst out laughing. Radius knew that at times Emma berated herself for her size 16 figure. But as a friend, she knew the whole story. And just wished that the guys Emma met would get to know her for her personality and not her outward appearance. Emma's tragic car crash that took her brother's life caused her to fall into a deep depression, and now that' she's forgiven herself, her minds whole again. But on the other hand, her body hasn't quite regulated from the trauma. But she had been working hard at it.

A shared Taxi:

The week had been long for Emma. The 45 year old fashion buyer had stayed up late last night

finishing up notes for tomorrow's meeting. They'd be discussing what all she'd be buying at the fashion convention she would be attending. At about midnight she managed to crawl into bed. Practically falling asleep before her head hit the pillows. The next morning, Emma woke up extra early to throw in the last of her things into the little overnighter to bring to work with her. It was another hectic and fun day at work Friday evening, which usually meant, she'd probably not get out of the office until pretty late again. So around 10:30pm she rushed out of the company conference meeting where she'd been with all the other colleagues hashing out the big weekend event in Dallas. Scooting into her office, she kicked off her heels and put on the low-loafers. Then she grabbed the carry on suitcase on wheels. Wheeling it out to the sidewalk, she'd hailed a taxi-cab.

"Whew…she said shivering. She'd opened the door to get in and to her surprise a handsome stranger opened the other door on the other side. "Oops, excuse me miss," the stranger said. "I'm in a hurry, but I'm sorry… I didn't mean to hail your taxi." "What a gentlemen," Emma thought to herself. "Oh no," she said. "I realize you didn't mean anything by it." "But if you don't mind, I am also in a hurry." "Where to," he asked? … "The airport," she replied. "Well that's good - me too," his brilliant eyes lit up!

"Hmm... maybe it's just our lucky day and we can share it." Now he might've thought she was talking about the cab, but it went deeper than that with Emma. She believed somehow they'd share the whole day. So they both jumped into the taxi and headed to the airport, where they made small talk. "Thanks for sharing your ride with me; I'm Elliott Jenkins, nice to meet you!" "Certainly Elliott, I'm Emma Oliver." Then she felt a click on the inside and knew this was it. In fact, she'd forgotten all about the woes of never

finding her one true love, when she met Elliott. When she thought of him, all her apprehensions just left. This man didn't make her feel self conscious about her size or who she was. At the same time, when she stared at him, he reminded her of a lovely- shiny- knight who'd come to rescue her in a nick of time. Who knew that these two strangers rushing through life in such a busy city would find each other bumping into a cab? And who'd have guessed that Ms. Emma's warm hearted pot of generosity would be topped off by a casual toned handsome stranger, so to speak? "So…ooo, where's your flight headed to," Elliott dared to ask? She admired that he even cared. I'm a designer buyer for Ann Taylor Fashions, and I've got a show to attend to in Dallas," she told the nice man. "Wow...Isn't that incredible," he slightly laughed. "What," she looked curious. "It's just that … I'm heading to Dallas as well," he said.

Emma new this was no coincidence. Looking at Elliott for a silent moment she knew someone upstairs had saw her past anguish. Someone knew she needed this breath of fresh air in her life right now. And with both of them, nothing seemed awkward. Looking up at one another, it was like their minds were on the same wave-length. Then Emma broke the silence between them. "I wonder if," … "We're on the same flight." Elliott had finished her sentence. "Cool," she said grinning. Following that little Déjà vu, Emma turned her head towards the window, looked out, and whispered … "Thank you god." Yes indeed she was grateful. After having suffered through a month and a half of horrible blind dates, she was very thankful to have met Elliot Jenkins. And he, well … it turns out that … "Elliott was pretty crazy about Emma Oliver." Cause not only was she good for him, but she had the

same goals and values."

STORY FOURTEEN

LOVES MISSION

"The Lord spoke to Tamika and told her Christopher Paul was HIS promise to her of a husband. "

It was the middle of the week and Tamika Provo was just about to set her feet on American soil again. She'd been out of town overseas on a missionary journey with some other college students. As the small plane smoothly transported the passengers on the last leg of their journey, Tamika closed her eyes and braced herself. She'd been afraid of flying since she was a little girl. She didn't know why man's natural airplanes and helicopter's brought so much fear to her mind! But she'd always boasted of being ready to fly away home to be with Jesus when he did come back. Tamika was only 23 and now she was a sophomore in college. She loved the African Native People. She felt God wanted her to be a missionary to those poor loving children and their mothers. In fact, she was sure of it. Raised in the hill country of Austin Texas, she understood all about ministry pursuits. Her Father, Smith was a Bishop of the United Churches of

Austin. And her mom, well she was the best saint you could find on earth. In Tamika's eyes her mother was a real 'Mother Teresa.' This desperation inside her about serving God brought with it much apprehension and joy. And soon after graduation she had planned to start her new life to the country of Africa. Unfortunately, there was only one thing missing. Though Tamika understood she couldn't plan something like this, she desired to have a companion alongside her when she started this African journey.

In her heart, she'd already said yes to God's call on her life, back in high school. Now she wasn't a teenager anymore and her passion, along with a need to get the intern grade had sent her to Kenya Africa to get a little taste of what life and ministry would be like there. She recalls how intensely hot, smelly and poor the country was. It had been her heightened

insecurities that had enveloped the excitement of her return. So today disembarking from the plan, she inhaled the freshness of the Texas air and viewed her hometown land with a new found appreciation. But her heart still ached for those poor little babies and children she'd left back in Kenya. Standing there on the green patchy grass absorbing all she could, Tamika heard the Lord's voice speak to her. He told her by the time she graduated from college; He will have sent her a husband. Looking up at the other passengers congregated around the plane, Tamika kept looking for the person who'd spoken to her. Though in doubt for just a moment, she really already knew no human man had spoken to her. But that it was the Lord. For Tamika, this was a first. God had never spoken to her in an audible voice.

Why was it that she felt such an urge to mission in Kenya of all places? Here she was a gorgeous red-

headed, freckled-face, ivory-skinned white female, who didn't look like she belonged there. So she continued to view her home town land and soil. The land was sparse and spread out for miles and miles. There was plenty of it to go around. It was beautiful and plenty if nothing else. Equally, standing among the noisy lot of people, a bunch of them like her, hadn't claimed their luggage yet. Tamika tried her best to block out the surrounding commotion. All she could think about was what had just happened with the audible voice and all she could see in her mind were the barren lands filled with dirt and not enough food, the children dying, and mothers loss of emotions because of not being able to nurse their babies. The sight was nothing to be compared from there to here in Tamika's home town. There she'd observed graves and the stench of poverty. Here at home she viewed majestic hills and towering evergreens, and the happiness of having enough.

Indeed, she'd never known what it was like ever to go hunger for one night - or to fear for your very life because of gorilla warfare. Then tears shot to her eyes. Tamika recanted the many graves – that sat on many a dirt hill, she'd seen while in Kenya. Her heart felt full of hurt for the foreign people. Then Tamika remembered why it was, that she'd felt such deep calling. It was the story and yet another sight of another man, who'd, walked down a long dusty road toward death. But this man carried a load for the whole world as he kept trying to fit the cross evenly on his back. Tamika saw it so clearly, and now she knew. No one or nothing could stop her from going forward to love these beautiful broken people. It was the picture of a man who'd been strung up on the same piece of wood he'd carried up that spacious hill where people stood watching to see what he'd do to rescue himself. It was the remembrance of His torn, abused and bleeding body that settled it for Tamika

that early evening, on Austin Texas soil.

It was now June 27th and the hot sweltering sticky weather only raised the excitement in the Texas air. The arena was full. Parents and relatives were everywhere. It looked like a carnival, rodeo or some kind of gun show. Moving along, the college students took their places in the stands to sing the American Anthem. Tamika, now 28 years old, stood tall and somewhat nervous looking out at her parents taking pictures of her professors and all the staff teachers. Her mother would be building an album to send with her overseas. But still Tamika could hardly believe it. Her life had been so busy and full, that she had lost track of time. Was she really graduating college? Had eight years gone by already, she questioned. Coming out with a Doctors degree was a plus. She was now ready to serve in a medical capacity in Kenya Africa.

But it all seemed unreal, that Tamika pinched her beautiful ivory-girl-face. Which by now had turned a bright shade of red, with an additional hundred or more freckles added, due to standing out on the metal bleachers beneath the blinding sun. Then suddenly, her mind scrambled back to the Lord's promise about a husband companion to accompany her to Africa. But the scary thing was she'd not met him yet - at least not to her knowledge. Then again, she recalled her promise to God to do her journey no matter what. She knew she'd grown up with much and was just thankful for the opportunity to give back. She saw her mom and dad trust God at very high levels of faith. So she figured she wasn't but a piece of dough being cut by the same cookie cutter.

Likewise, she kept to her ramblings during the graduation ceremony. Until, surprisingly, she heard an unusual sound. It was the horn's blowing that

brought her quickly out of her isolated world alone, back into the crowded stand. The College Dean, 'Mr. Shaanklin,' had called forth a young man by the name of Christopher Paul. He looked to be about 30 to 32 years old. He was dressed in a neatly grey tailored suit, and had on a pair of black Texas rawhide boots. "Who was this astute and dashing man," she thought. The Dean handed over the microphone to Christopher Paul. When he opened his mouth to greet the audience and college graduates, Tamika noticed an unusual nod her way. She followed his big green eyes everywhere he glanced. Intrigued by his mannerism, she kept watching with a slight smile. Then it happened again, The Lord spoke to her and told her Christopher Paul was HIS promise to her, of a husband. She didn't say anything, but she did wonder at how in the world this same young man speaking at the podium would be her husband. "What Lord?" she commented. Looking forward as if nothing had just

happened, Tamika tried to put it out of her mind, but she couldn't. Every other word or so she looked up at Christopher, standing on the stage speaking, and then she'd look down at the open-toed strappy-gold shoes that poked out from under her Purple Gown with Gold trim. Again through all the commotion Tamika had heard the Lord's voice. This time it wasn't audible as the first time. But it appeared to be coming from her heart-area. While it is true she'd already taken a liking to this bold, humbly-dashing man. At the same time, she didn't know what to think. So she tried not to. "Can we give this young man a hand everybody?" Mr. Shaanklin said… securing the microphone again, to continue the ceremony. "Some of you may not know him. But Christopher is one of our finest students from right here at our home University. He's a graduate of honors. He walked across this same stage four years ago as an honor roll student, with two major scholarships, one in medicine and the other in political foreign missions. I'm honored to say he's now serving as the American Ambassador to Kenya Africa.

It had been an hour now, since Christopher had taken his seat. And finally, everyone had been called to walk across the outdoor stage except Tamika. And since her last name was 'Zellman,' of course she'd be the last person marching across those floors to receive her 'Diploma/Certificate' of Graduation. Then again, Mr. Shaanklin spoke. "While it is in the nature of most people, to talk about themselves, Tamika Zellman seemed to be the exception," He said. "At the same time, it had been brought to my and other staff member's attention, all the good Miss Tamika has done for the college and its surrounding community." "So Folks....while we're very proud of all our students, who've done a great job in finishing their education with honors." "I'd like you all to put your hands together in congratulating this very fine student,

Miss Tamika Zellman." While everybody was clapping and snapping pictures, Tamika's friends and family members whistled her hoorahs. God had blessed her royally today. Furthermore, little had she noticed that Dean Shaanklin had called forth Christopher again - He stood there facing her with a bouquet of roses in his arm and another piece of paper of sorts all rolled up! Dean Shaanklin continued speaking… "When we found out that Tamika had been going throughout the community feeding little kids on the streets and taking them to the library to study reading on her off campus days, we knew then this young woman had a gift she'd already started to use for the Lord." "Then I found out that after her graduation, she too, would be serving as a Doctor to families in Kenya Africa." "Nothing more could make what we do here at this college, so rewarding. By now with all the humbling honors, God's presence had fallen and there was hardly a dry eye in the place. Even Mr. Shaanklin had

a quiver in his voice. "And you now it folks…one good deed deserves another, he said with hinting happiness." "So I went ahead and called in my secret weapon, Christopher Paul." Similarly, I want to say thanks to everyone who participated in the nomination of Miss Tamika Zellman, for a Foreign Scholarship in the amount of $50,000.00!" At first, Tamika stood frozen in her tracks with her mouth dropped wide open. Secondly, tears filled her bright eyes; as she moved in close to receive her rewards. Then, the two of them, Christopher and Tamika, stood on the stage hand in hand.

- *END* -

Of Loves

Melting

Pot

We hope you enjoyed this compilation of Christian based inspirational light romance stories. To read more inspiring and creative works by the author, or to get Christian self help books and resources see authors spot light at: www.icreateinspiration.com or see author's spotlight at: http://www.lulu.com/spotlight/confidentpeople

www.ingramcontent.com/pod-product-compliance
Ingram Content Group UK Ltd.
Pitfield, Milton Keynes, MK11 3LW, UK
UKHW041936190726
13854UKWH00004B/1628